Surrogacy Helps Make a Family Grow!

Written by Sharon LaMothe & Tina Rella
Illustrated by Monica Meza

I dedicate this book to my children, Tony and Erika, for being my wonderful inspiration and constant reminders of the joys of parenting. You both are why I wanted to pass along the gift of life to those who took a leap of faith and trusted me with their most treasured dreams. You are my world!

To my husband Joe: You are a remarkable man who has supported me and the families we helped throughout both of my surrogate journeys. It would not have been nearly as rewarding if I didn't have you to share each special and wondrous moment! I love you!

To all of the women with whom I have had the pleasure to meet and who have put their heart and souls into helping build families via surrogacy: You are the real heroes! Without your commitment, dedication, and open minded point of view there would be no surrogacy! And to those just starting out on your surrogacy journey...You are changing lives and adding a branch to some lucky Intended Parents family tree. You are making dreams come true!

-Sharon LaMothe

One sunny summer day, the Johnsons decided to go to the park. As Tony, Jessica, and Erika were having a great time playing in the sand, Mom and Dad sat together and watched them.

They noticed a couple sitting alone on a nearby bench looking a little sad.

"We are so lucky to have our wonderful children," said Dad. "I can't imagine our lives without them."

"I know," Mom replied, looking at the couple. "Some people aren't as lucky as we are."

That evening Mom and Dad couldn't stop thinking about that couple they saw at the park earlier and how sorry they felt for them. Then, Mom had a great idea.

"What if I offered to carry a baby for a couple who needs my help?" she asked.

Dad agreed that this was exactly what they should do.

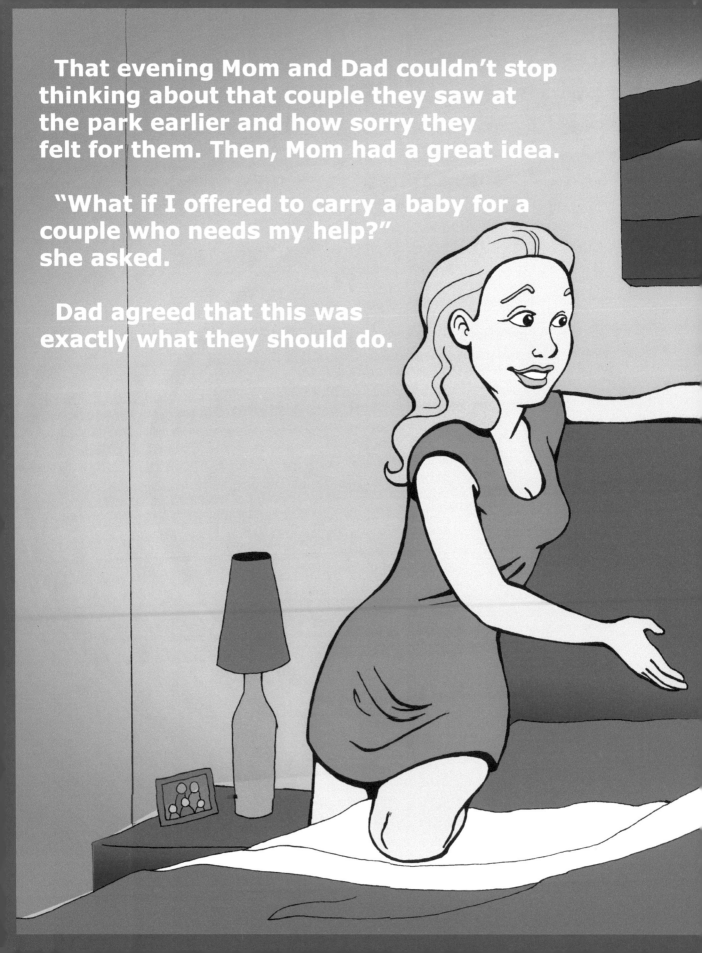

The next month, after thinking it through and doing lots of research on becoming a Surrogate, Mom and Dad decided to visit a surrogacy agency, where they met with a wonderful lady named Mrs. Donaldson. She explained how their surrogacy program worked and even had a loving couple in mind for them.

"Can you come back next week to meet them?"
asked Mrs. Donaldson.
"Of course! We would love to!" said Mom excitedly.
"We hope we can help make another family
as happy as we are," smiled Dad.

At the agency the following week, Mrs. Donaldson introduced Mom and Dad to the nice couple that needed help starting a family of their own. Their names were Mr. & Mrs. Davis, and they wanted a baby for a very long time.

Everyone sat down together and shared their stories. They agreed that they would love to work together and help the Davis' have the baby they always wanted.

That evening, after dinner, Mom sat with Tony on the couch.

"Tony, how would you feel if Mommy helped another Mommy & Daddy have a baby of their own?"

"Who are they? Do I know them?" asked Tony.

"See, the Mommy would use her eggs and the Daddy uses his sperm to make an embryo," said Mom. "When it is ready, the doctor will put the embryo inside my uterus so that it can grow into a little baby."

"So, the baby is going to be ours? I don't want another little sister!" exclaimed Tony.

"No honey!" chuckled Mom. "That baby will belong to its parents, Mr. and Mrs. Davis. We will just be helping them start their family. It will be our gift to them."

"Oh," Tony considered. "Well I guess that sounds okay."

"The doctor says that the embryos look great! We saw them under the microscope. It looks like we're ready for you!"

Dr. Williams was about to transfer the embryo into Mom's uterus so that she could carry the baby for nine months until he's born.

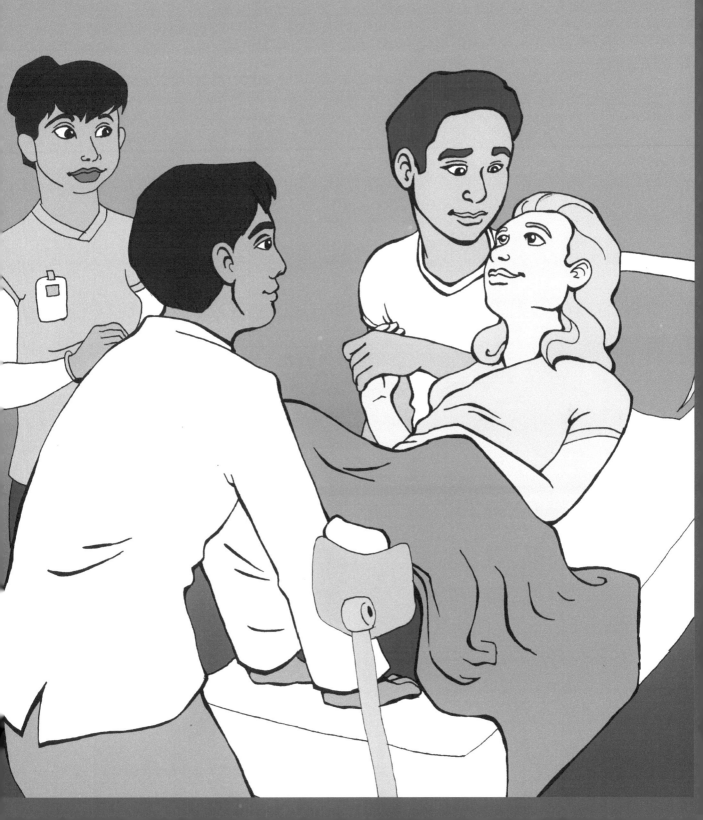

"You'll do great, honey!" smiled Dad.
"We can't thank you enough for even trying
this for us!" said Mrs. Davis.
"Now for the two week wait!" added Mr. Davis.

One day, a couple of months later, while Mom and Jessica were at the store, Jessica noticed that Mom's belly was starting to grow. "You have a baby in there?" asked Jessica.

"Yes, I do, honey. But it's not "our" baby ~ I'm just taking care of him until he's ready to come out. Once he's born, his Mommy & Daddy can hold him and love him, just like Daddy & I love you and your brother and sister." explained Mom.

" So, I will still be your baby, Mommy?" she wondered.

" You will always be my baby," smiled Mom as she gave Jessica a big hug.

One day Erika was playing with her best friend,
Jasmine, who commented, "You didn't tell me your Mom
was going to have another baby!"

"Yep, but the baby isn't ours," explained Erika.
"My mom is helping another family by carrying their baby
because the Mommy isn't able to. When he's born,
he will go home with his own Mommy and Daddy"

"You mean your Mom is giving away your little brother?"
asked Jasmine.

"No, he's not OUR baby brother. The doctor put an embryo
that belonged to Mr. and Mrs. Davis inside my Mommy
so it could grow into a baby. It's really cool that we can
help someone have a family like ours." said Erika.

"Wow! And you won't have to change his diapers!"
Jasmine laughed.

After several months, Mom was ready to have Mr. & Mrs. Davis' baby. Everyone met at the hospital and was so excited about the new baby's arrival. The doctor helped Mom as she started to give birth. After a while, out he came ~ a healthy little baby boy.

Everyone was so happy and Mom was very tired! "Now our family is complete! Thank you for making all our dreams come true!" said Mrs. Davis joyfully.

About a year later, the Johnsons received an invitation in the mail from the Davis' that read:

CAN'T WAIT TO SEE YOU AT JAKE'S

FIRST BIRTHDAY
PARTY!

We are so happy!
Thank you everyone
for helping us
make our family!

CPSIA information can be obtained
at www.ICGtesting.com
Printed in the USA
LVHW072250201222
735671LV00019B/127